孔子故乡全览

THE WHOLE   VIEW CONFUCIUS

孔子像 Statue of Confucius

孔子像 Statue of Confucius

前　言

"南沂西泗绕晴霞，北岱东蒙拥翠华。"

驰名中外的历史文化名城曲阜，古称圣域贤关，是中华民族始祖先皇的发祥地，殷商故都，周、汉鲁国都城。春秋末期著名思想家、政治家、教育家、儒家学派创始人孔子的故乡。

"千年礼乐归东鲁，万古衣冠拜素王。"孔子诞生于尼山，成长于阙里，设教于杏坛，出仕于鲁都，归葬于泗上，在曲阜留下了众多的活动遗迹，后人又兴建了许多纪念建筑。至汉武帝"罢黜百家，独尊儒术"时，孔子的学术思想得到空前光大，成为后世历代王朝治理国家的正统思想，儒家祖庭曲阜孔庙成为列入国家祀典的礼制庙宇。历经百余次工程，多次大规模扩建，到明正德八年（公元1513年）"移县城卫庙"形成孔庙雄距城中的布局，清代建筑改用黄色琉璃瓦、金龙和玺彩绘，是我国礼制规格最高的庙宇之一。

"与国咸休安富尊荣公府第，同天并老文章道德圣人家"。孔子嫡孙是中国封建社会中世袭贵族地位历史最久的贵族世家。历代封建王朝在尊崇孔子儒家思想时，为显示崇德报功，对孔子嫡孙一再封爵。明洪武十年（公元1377年）五十六代衍圣公奉敕创建独立的衍圣公府，明弘治十六年（1503年）进行扩建，形成了现在孔府的规模。

孔子死后，葬鲁城北泗上，子孙接冢而葬。历代王朝为褒扬儒学，不断增拓墓园，辟神道，筑周垣，建林门，使孔林成为世界上延时最久的家族墓地。

"有朋自远方来不亦乐乎"！曲阜，举世驰名的东方圣城、热情好客的孔子故乡人民热烈欢迎前来观览胜地的中外嘉宾！

编　者

PREFACE

Qufu, a world known historical and cultural city, was named a sacred place for kings and sages in ancient time. It is the birthplace of earliest ancestors and ancient emperors of the Chinese nation, the capital of Shang Dynasty and capital of State Lu in Zhou and Han Dynasty, also the hometown of Confucius, the famous thinker, statesman, educator, founder of Confucianism in the late time of the Spring and Autumn Period.

Confucius left many vestiges in Qufu. He was born here in Nishan, grew up in Queli, preached his beliefs on the Altar of Apricot, got involved in the politics in the Capital of Lu and was buried by the Sishui River. Many buildings have been constructed by posterity in memory of him. Since Emperor Wu of the Han Dynasty adopted the policy of recanting all schools of thoughts and respecting only Confucianism. Confucianism had become the legitimate ideology of Chinese feudal society and its place of origin, Confucius Temple of Qufu, has been in the list of temples being worshipped nationwide. The temple had been enlarged many times and undergone hundreds of construction work. In 1513, the town was moved to guard the temple. Hence the layout of Confucius Temple lying in the center of Qufu city came into being. In the Qing Dynasty, the temple was rebuilt with yellow glazed tiles and decorated, which made it become one of the temples of highest architectural form to the criterion of China feudal society.

On the gate of Confucius Residence, there is a couplet to the effect that the Confucius family is the most respectable family in China and that essays and virtues originated from this family will be long lasting. The direct line of Confucius family was the noble family of longest history in China feudal society. While worshipping Confucius and spreading Confucianism, emperors of various dynasties offered high posts and other favors to Confucius descendants to boast Confucius contributions to the feudal system. In 1377 of Ming Dynasty, the 56th Lord Yansheng built a separate residence under emperor's order. In 1503, the residence was enlarged and thus the size of the Confucius Residence laid out.

After his death, Confucius was buried in the north area of Qufu by Sishui River, and later his descendants were buried beside his tomb. Emperors of different dynasties after him had Confucius Mausoleum enlarged many times, the celestial path paved and surrounding walls and gate built. All of these make Confucius Mausoleum become a family cemetery which last for longest time in the world.

Confucius said: Isn't great to have friends come from afar! Qufu is a world famous east holy city. The hospitable people of Confucius's hometown welcome friends from home and abroad to visit Qufu.

World Cultural Heritage-Historical Relics of Qufu, Hometown of Confucius

孔庙景点方位图

Map of Confucius Temple

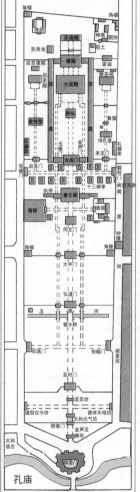

孔庙

1. Gateway of striking the Golden Bell & Beating Jade
2. Gate of Lattice star
3. Gateway of Universal Vitality
4. Gateway of Succeeding Dec trines
5. Gateway of Pervading Virtues
6. Gateway ofthe temple of Satint
7. Gate of saint Time
8. Gate of Looking up to heaven
9. Ga Archway of watchtower
11. Bridge of Green Jade River
12. Pavilion of Stone Man of Han Dynasty
13. The Green Jade River
14. Gate of Enhancing Morals
15. Great Middle Gate
16. Watchtowers
17. Watchtowers
18. Tongwen Gate
19. Western Courtyard(Zhai Su)
20. Eastern Courtyard(Zhai Su)
21. Kuiwen pavilion
22. Pavilion of the Thirteen Tablets
23. Pavilion of Imperial Tablets
24. Gate of Guan De
25. Gate of Former Residence of Confucius
26. Gate of Enlightening Saint
27. Gate of Intergratioin
28. Gate of Succeeding Saint
29. Storing place for gifts
30. The Eastern Side Room
31. The Western Side Room
32. Hall of Jing Si
33. Hall of Songs and Rites
34. The Former Well in the Former Residence
35. Altar of Apricot
36. Hall of Integration
37. Hall of Enlightening Saint
38. Hall of Worshipping Ancestors
39. Hall of Bedroom
40. Hall of Back Enlightening Saint
41. Family Temple
42. Silk Burning Stone
43. Hou Tu
44. Hall of Great Deeds
45. Great Chef
46. Great Butcher
47. Watchtowers

孔　庙

　　孔庙是祭祀春秋思想家、教育家、政治家孔子的庙宇。位于山东曲阜市旧城中心，原为历代祭孔之地，今为全国重点文物保护单位。现今孔庙是明清两代完成的，其建筑仿皇宫之制，前后九进落院，贯空于南北中轴线上，南北长1.3公里，占地327.5亩。有门坊54座，房屋466间，古树1700余株。周匝垣墙，配以角楼，院内苍松翠柏、森然排列，殿宇雕梁画栋、金碧辉煌，小桥流水，飞禽低旋，别有意境。庙内各类碑刻2000余块，为我国罕见的大型碑林之一。这样一组气魄宏大的古建筑群，时间之久远，保存之完好，其盛名享誉海内外。

Confucius Temple

　　Located in the center of the old city of Qufu, the Confucius Temple is a place of temple for people to offer scarifies to Confucius, the philospher, educator and politician in the Spring and Autumn Period.The temple used to be a place of making sacrifices to Confucius, and now it became a historic site under special protection by the government.Today's Confucius Temple was completed in Ming and Qing dynasties.The whole complex was modeled on the imperial palace with many courtyards and on the north-south axes.It is 1.3 kilometers long from north to south and the whole complex covers an area of 327.5 ares.There are 54 archways,466 rooms, and many halls,pavilions and chambers.Encircled the complex is the wall with watchtowers on each corner.Inside pine trees lined,along with splendid halls,beautiful paintings,exquisite bridges and chirping birds.There are more than 2,000 tablets of various kind.These well-preserved tablets are rare ones in China and enjoy good fame at home and abroad and attract thousands of tourists to visit and worship.

万仞宫墙　曲阜正南门，古时只有皇帝及钦差大臣来曲阜祭孔时，此门才打开。"万仞宫墙"四字为清乾隆帝所书。

Gate of Respecting the Saint

The south gate of Qufu was only opened when the Emperor and Imperial envoy come to The Residence of the confucius. "Gate of Respecting the Saint" was written by Qianlong Emperor.

金声玉振坊

进孔庙的起点，明嘉靖十七年（公元1538年）建，三间四柱式石坊，额坊刻明人胡缵宗题"金声玉振"四字。孟子曰："孔子之谓集大成。集大成也者，金声而玉振之也。"以象征孔子思想集古圣先贤之大成，如同奏乐，以金钟发声，以玉磬收韵，集众音之大成一样。

Gateway of Striking Golden Bell & Beating Jade

It is the starting point to enter the Confucius Temple and was buit in Ming Emperor Jiajing's year.It is a three-room, four-pillar stone gateway,with inscriptions of four Chinese characters."Jin Sheng Yu Zhen" (The sound of gold and beating jade).Menfucius said : "Confucius preaches culmination of all that is good, which is compared to striking the gold and beating the jade" .Confucius succeeded all good thoughts of the saints before him,which is very much like startig by sounding golden bells and ending by beating jade instrument and reaching a culmination of various music.

灵星门　Gate of Lattice Star

太和元气坊 明嘉靖二十三年（公元 1544 年）建，三间四柱石坊，山东巡抚曾铣书额。"太和元气"是赞誉孔子的学术思想如同太空天体，循环往复、永恒长存。

Gateway of Universal vitality(Tai He Yuan Qi Fang)

The three-room,four-pillar stone gateway was built in the year 1544 with its tablet written by Zeng Xian,governor of Shangdong at that time.

"The Universal Vitality" means that the thoughts of Confucius is recycling and immortal just like the space and stars.

至圣庙坊 明代建筑，汉白玉三间四柱坊。原名宣圣庙坊，清雍正七年（公元1729年）易为今名。

Gateway to the temple of Saint

It was built in Ming dynasty. The two-room, four-pillar marble stone gateway got its name in the year 1729.

天龙
The Heavenly Dragon

德侔天地坊
Gateway of Pervading virtues

道冠古今坊 Gateway of Succeeding Doctrines

　　此两坊均建于明永乐十三年（公元1415年），三间四柱、双重飞檐、六层斗式。东西两侧相对而建，是孔庙第一道腰门.

　　"德侔天地、道冠古今"是赞美孔子之德与天地齐，他的学说古今无二。

　　The two gateways were built in Ming dynasty.They are three-room,tour-pillar and double eaves buildings.

　　The eastern and western part were the first side gate to the Confucius Temple.

　　"The pervading of Virtues and Succeeding of Doctrines" means that Confucius's virtues pervades the whole universe and his doctrines is unparalleled in the world.

璧水桥　明永乐十三年(公元 1445 年)建,砖石券拱桥三座。一水横穿,碧波涣涣,水壅绕如璧,故名"璧水"。桥因水而名,曰"璧水桥"。

Bridge of Green Jade River

　　The three-arch stone bridge was built in the year 1445.The river running under the bridge is as green as jade,hence the name Green Jade River.

圣时门陛石
Staircases of Gate of Saint Time.

弘道门 孔庙第三道大门。始建于明洪武十年（公元 1377 年）系当时的孔庙大门。

Gate of Enhancing Morals

    The third gate of the Confucius Temple and first built in Ming Emperor Hongwu's time. It was the main gate at that time.

大中门　　孔庙第四道大门，始建于金大定年间，宋以前系孔庙第一道大门，后经明弘治时扩建，今门系清代所建。五间三门，原名中和门，后改为大中门，清乾隆帝御书门匾。

The Great Middle Gate

The fourth gate of the Confucius Temple and first built in Jin Dynasty. It was the first gate to the Confucius Temple before Song Dynasty. Later it was renovated in Ming Dynasty and today's gate was built in Qing Dynasty. The five-room, three-door gate was originally named The Middle Peace Gate and later it was changed into The Great Middle Gate With Qing Emperor Qianlong's inscriptions on it.

同文门 孔庙第五道大门。始建于北宋初期，系当时孔庙大门。清初名参同门，雍正八年（公元 1730 年）世宗钦命为"同文门"，乾隆题写门匾。

Tong wen Gate

It is the fifth gate to the Confucius Temple and was first built in the early North Song Dynasty and was the main gate then. It was named Gate of Cantong, and the name was changed into Gate of Tongwen in the year 1730 with Qing Emperor Qianlong's inscriptions on it.

角楼   孔庙角楼共4座，分别位于大中门两侧墙角和庙东北角、西北角。始建于元至顺二年（公元1331年），后经历代重修。角楼建在庙墙拐角的高台上，台之内侧有马道供上下。此四个角楼构成一个防卫屏障，显示出孔庙如皇宫一样的威严。

The Watchtowers

     There are four watchtowers in the Confucius Temple, situated two sides of the Great Middle Gate and the northeast and northwest corner of the temple. They were first built in Yuan Dynasty and had been renovated many times. The four watchtowers were built on the high stand in the corners with a path inside for people to climb up and descend. The four watchtowers constitute a defense works, showing the dignity like that of the imperial palaces.

奎文阁 始建于宋天禧二年（公元 1018 年），始名藏书楼。金章宗在明昌二年（公元 1191 年）扩建时改名"奎文阁"，清乾隆帝重新题匾额。古以奎星为二十八宿之一，主文章，后人把孔子比作天上奎星，故以此名之。奎文阁为历代帝王赐书、墨迹收藏之处，它独特的建筑结构，又是中国古代著名楼阁之一。

The Kuiwen Pavilion

First built in the year 1018 and named Tower of Collections of Books, is was named again Kuiwen Pavilion in 1191 during its renovation with Qing Emperor Qianlongs writings. It is the place where emperors displayed and preserved theri handwritings and is also a famous pavilion for its unique architecture.

成化碑

　　明宪宗御制重修孔庙碑。明成化四年（公元1468年）立。碑高6.2米。龟趺高1.25米。碑文为宪宗朱见深御制，字楷书，书体严谨、端庄。为世人所称道，是明代名碑之一。

The Chenghua Tablet

It was erected in Ming dynasty by Ming Emperor Xianzong. The tablet is 6.2 meters high and the base is 1.25 meters high. The rigorous and dignified regular inscriptions ,written by Ming Emperor Xiangzong, Were well acclaimed by people.

金碑亭　为孔庙中最早的古建筑。
Pavilion of Gold Tablet
　　One of the thirteen tablet pavilions, is the eldest building in the Temple of Confucius.

十三碑亭　The Thirteen Tablet Pavilions

大成门   十三碑亭北，五门并列，居中一门名大成门，"大成"是孟子对孔子的评价，赞颂孔子达到了集古圣先贤之大成的至高境界。

Gate of Integration(Da Cheng Men)

North of the thirteen tablets pavilions .There are five gates. The one in the middle in called Gate of integration, and is also the seventh gate to the Confucius Temple, It is roofed by yellow glazed tile."Da Cheng", is what Menfucius viewed Confucius. It means that Confucius had integrated all that was good of people before him.

勾心・斗角　　由于大成门南端的十三碑亭系由金代以来逐代增建而成。能工巧匠们充分运用传统的"勾心・斗角"的建筑手法，巧妙地解决了建筑结构空间的问题。

Gou Xin and Dou Jiao

As the thirteen tablet pavilions to the south end of Gate of Integration were built one by one since Jin Dynasty, the skilled architects had been enough in solving the space issues between various structures with the so called traditional techniques such as Gou Xin and Dou Jiao.

先师手植桧

位于大成门内石阶东侧。古桧挺拔高耸，树冠如盖。据记载，古桧原为孔子亲手所植，几经枯荣毁于火难。今存桧树为清雍正十年（公元 1732 年）于古树桩下复生的新枝长成的。树东有明人杨光训"先师手植桧"刻文石碑。"先师手植桧"被人们视为孔子思想和孔子后裔兴衰的象征，倍受敬仰。

The Juniper Planted by the Deceased Master

It is located to the east of the stone stairs inside Gate of Integration. It is recorded that the towering juniper was planted by Confucius and had been destroyed in fire many times.Today's juniper was grown in Qing Emperor Yong zhengs time. To the east of the tree is a tablet with writings by Yang Guangxun of Ming Dynasty.

杏檀藻井
Sunk Panel

杏坛 相传孔子讲学的地方,在此孔子向72弟子传授"六艺".

Altar of Apricot

　　Altar of Apricot was said to be the place where Confucius once delivered lectures to his 72 disciples.

大成殿 　孔庙内宫殿式主体建筑，也是孔庙的核心。唐代时称文宣王殿，为五间。宋天禧五年（公元1021年）大修时，移今址并扩为七间。宋崇宁三年（公元1104年）徽宗赵佶取《孟子》："孔子之谓集大成"语义，下诏更名为"大成殿"，清雍正二年（公元1724年）重建，九脊重檐，黄瓦覆顶，多式斗，雕梁画栋，斗八藻井饰以金龙和玺彩图，双重飞檐正中竖匾上刻清雍正皇帝御书"大成殿"三个贴金大字。殿高24.8米，长45.69米，宽24.85米，座落在2.1米高的殿基上，为全庙最高建筑，也是中国三大古殿之一。

Hall of Integration

It is the main hall and also the center of the Confucius Temple, There were five rooms in Tang dynasty and it was called Hall of Wen Xuan Wang. In the year 1021 when it was rebuilt, it was moved to today's site and was expanded to seven rooms, it was named Hall of Integration in 1104 by Song Emperor Huizong as he cited a quotation from Menfucius to the effect that Confucius integrated all that is good before him. The hall was rebuilt in the year 1724 by Qing Emperor Yongzheng. The whole magnificent hall, roofed by glazed tiles, had the Emperor Yongzheng's writings in the middle, and is the highest building in the Confucius Temple.

螭首
The Outgoing Eaves on the Terrace of Hall of Integration

孔庙大成殿孔子像
Statue of Confucius in
the Hall of Integration

檐柱

是曲阜建筑的一个特点,而大成殿的石檐柱最有代表性。殿周 28 根独石雕成的擎檐柱高达 6 米,直径 0.8 米,下饰莲花柱础。左、右、后檐下 18 根石柱,皆为八菱形水磨浅雕团龙,每柱雕龙 72 条。前檐 10 柱,为深浮雕双龙戏珠,衬以波涛,缀以山石。10 根龙柱两两相对,造型精美,雕刻剔透,为域内罕见,据说清乾隆帝来曲阜祭拜孔子时,石柱均用红绫包裹,不敢让皇帝看到,恐怕皇帝会因其超过皇宫而怪罪。

The Pillars

One of the characteristics of the architecture of Confucius Temple if that the whole hall is supported by some stone pillars with sculptures on them.

寝殿 位于大成殿后，一座重檐大殿矗立，为孔庙三大主体建筑之一，是供奉孔子夫人亓官氏的祭殿。始建于宋天禧二年（公元1018年），明弘治十三年（公元1500年）扩建，清雍正八年（公元1730年）重修。

Hall of Bedroom

It is located behind the Hall of Integration and is the second largest building in the Confucius Temple and is the place to pay tribute ot the wife of Confucius, Lady Yuangong, It was first build in 1018 in Song Dynasty and was renovated in 1730 in Qing Dynasty.

诗礼堂 承圣门后第一进院落迎面五间正殿，名诗礼堂，是后世纪念孔子教育儿子孔鲤学《诗》学《礼》的地方。始建于宋代，原为宋真宗大中祥符元年（公元1008年）拜谒孔庙驻跸之所。明弘治十七年（公元1504年）重修扩建。清明时，圣祖、高宗祭祀孔子时曾在此听孔子后裔讲解经书。现展览石刻《孔子事迹图》。

Hall of Songs and Rites

Right inside the Gate of Succeeding the Saint are five halls named Hall of Songs and Rites and are the places where the son of Confucius, Kongli studied The Songs and the Rites. In 1504 it Was iebuiit and renovated. Emperors of early Qing Dynasty once Listened to the explanations of Songs and Rites here by the descendants of Confucius. Now exhibited here is the Paintings of the Deeds of Confucius.

孔宅故井 据传为孔子当年的吃水井，位于诗礼堂后。井深3米，明中期以雕花石栏围护，内立明代"孔宅故井"碑。井水"既清且渫"，被称为"圣水"。

The Former Well in the Former Residence

The well, which was said to be the place where Confucius drank water, is located behind the Hall of Songs and Rites. It is three meters deep and was protected by stone balustrades since Ming Dynasty and with a tablet inside. The water is both clear and sweet hencemeriting the name "the Saint water." In the year 1748, Qing Emperor Qianlong established a pavilion to its west.

鲁壁 故井东有一壁孤立，形同照壁，壁前石碑上刻隶书"鲁壁"。秦始皇焚书时，孔子九代孙子孔鲋将《论语》《尚书》《礼记》《春秋》《孝经》等儒家经书，藏于孔子故宅墙中。明代为纪念孔鲋藏书的功绩而制鲁壁碑。

The Wall of Lu

East of the well stands an isolated wall, very much like a screen wall. In front of the wall erects a tablet with two Chinese characters "Lu Bi" (Wall of Lu) in the official script form inscribed within. When Emperor Qin Shihuang burned down all schools of books, the ninth generation of Confucius, Kong Fu hid all the Confucius classics such as The Analects, the Shangshu, the Book of Rites and the Book of Spring and Autumn in the wall of the former residence.In Ming Dynasty, the wall was erected in memory of Kong Fu's contribution of keeping these books.

钟楼 Bell Tower

鼓楼 Drum Tower

阙里坊 Queli Arch

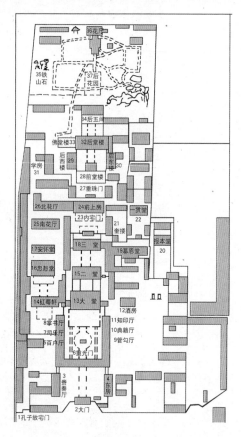

Map of Confucius Residence
1.Door of Former Residence of Confucius
2.Gate of Residence of the Saint
3.Hall of Submitting the roposals
4.Room of east side 5.Hall of hundred Household
6.Gate of Double light 7.Si Yue Hall 8.Zhangshu Hall
9.Guan Gou Hall 10.Hall of Ancientbooks and records
11.Hall of Recognizing the Seal 12.Cellar of liquor
13.The MainHall 14.Chamber of Red Calyx 15.The Second Hall
16.Hall of Fide lity & Genersity 17.Hall of conciliation
18.The Third Hall 19.Hall of cherishing the Benevolence
20.Hall of Delivering a records 21.Kui Chamber
22.Hall of Concistence 23.Gate of Inner Residence
24.Front MainHall 25.South Flower Hall 26.North Flower Hall
27.Gate of Haning beads 28.Tower of Front Hal
29.Back of West Tower 30.Back of East Tower 31.Learning Room
32.Tower of BackHall 33.Buddist Tower 34.The Five Back Rooms
35.Garden of lron Hill 36.Foreign-Style Houses 37.Rear Garden

孔 府

　　孔府又称"衍圣公府"，位于孔庙东侧，有"天下第一家"之称，是孔子嫡系长期居住的府第，也是中国封建社会官衙与内宅合一的典型建筑。孔子死后，子孙后代世代居庙旁守庙看管孔子遗物，到北宋末期，孔氏后裔住宅已扩大到数十间，到金代，孔子后裔一直是住在孔庙东边。随着孔子后世官位的升迁和封爵的提高，孔府建筑不断扩大，至宋、明、清达到现在规模。现在孔府占地约7.4公顷，有古建筑480间，分前后九进院落，中、东、西三路布局。

Residence of the Confucius

　　Located in the east of the Confucius Temple, and merited the title of "The First Family in the World", the Residence of the Confucius, also named "Residence of Lord Yansheng", is the house of Zhangzhi, a lineal descendant of Confucius. The residence typically features the combined architecture of the official mansion and private house of China's feudal society. After the death of Confucius, his descents lived in the temple and guarded the relic. At the end of the North Song Dynasty, the residence of his descendants had been expanded to a large residence with dozens of rooms. In Jin Dynasty, the descendants of Confucius had lived in the east of the Confucius Temple. With the promotion of ranks in court and increase of stipends of his descents, the Residence of the Confucius was renovated for many times and took shape early in the Song, Ming and Qing Dynasties. Today the Residence of the Confucius covers an area of 7.4 hectares. with 480 ancient rooms in nine compounds with the middle, eastern and western paths as its layout.

圣府大门 　　为三间五檩悬山式建筑，匾书"圣府"二字，为明朝严嵩所书。门两边有对联一副"与国咸休安富尊荣公府第，同天并老文章道德圣人家"，其中"富"字少上面一点，寓"富贵无头"，"章"字一竖通到上面立字，寓"文章通天"，此联概括出千百年来"圣人家"的气派。

Gate of the Residence of the Saint

The three-room, five-purling gate is in the hanging style. In the middle of the gate there is a tablet of two Chinese characters "Shengfu" (Residence of the Saint), written by YanSong, a Prime Minister in Ming Dynasty. On the two sides of the door hangs an ingenious couplet which displays the talent of the Saint.

圣人之门
The gate of saint

重光门 又称仪门，四柱回梁，悬山肩挑，前后重花蕾各四朵，所以又称"垂花门"。明代建筑，此门只有迎接圣旨，重大盛典，才在礼炮声中打开。

Gate of Double Lights（Chong Guang Men）

The gate is also called Gate Ritual. Supported by four pillars and four beams, the gate is also called Halled Hall of Hanging Flowers because there hangs four blossoms in front of and behind the gate . Built in Ming Dynasty , the gate was opened only in the salvo on grand accoasions like receiving an imperial edict.

大堂
The Main Hall of the Residence.

大堂内仪仗

堂内两侧及后面陈列着一品爵位的仪仗，还有一些象征特权和封爵的红底金子官衔牌，称"十八块云牌銮驾"，如"袭封衍圣公""紫禁城骑马"等，每当衍圣公出行，皆有专人执掌，以示威严。

Insignia in the Main Hall of the Residence

Displayed in the hall is the insignia of the title of the first rank as well as some official boards which symbolize privileges and imperial stipends. When Lord Yansheng was out, the insignia was held by designated person to wield the dignity.

大堂内景 Inner View of the Main Hall of the Residence.

六厅

孔府仿照封建王朝的六部而设六厅，在二门以内两侧，分别为管勾厅、百户厅、典籍厅、司乐厅、知印厅、掌书厅，共同管理孔府事务。

The six hall

In the Residence at its two sides are flanked by six halls: Hall of GuanGou, Hall of Baihu, Hall of Dianji, Hall of Siyue, Hall of Zhiyin and Hall of Zhangshu which were modeled on the Six Ministries of a feudal dynasty to attend the affairs of the Confucius.

穿厅及阁老凳

与大堂、二堂相连，呈"工"字型。"阁老凳"传说为明代奸相严嵩在听说皇帝将要对其治罪时，托衍圣公代为求情时，坐候之物。

Hall of the Corridor and Bench for the Elder

The corridor links the Main Hall and Second Hall and takes the shape of "工". There is a story that when the treacherous Prime Minister, Yan Song heard that the Emperor would punish him for his crimes, he turned to the help of his relative, Lord Yansheng. Bench for the Elder was the place where Yan Song was sitting and waiting fidgetedly for Lord Yan-Sheng to intercede for him.

二堂内景 为衍圣公会见四品官以上官员宣示典章礼仪的地方。
Inner View of the Second Hall

The hall is the place where Lord Yan Sheng met official of forth and even higher rank officials.

三堂内景 也叫退厅，是处理家族内部纠纷和事务的地方。
Inner of the Third Hall

The hall is also called Tui Hall and is the Place where the internal disputes and affairs of the Confucius family were solved.

奎楼 明代四层方型砖结构建筑，为孔府最高建筑物。房内一层有三米多深水井一口，用盖板罩盖，外人不能进入，可以应付不测，作避难之用，实际上是孔府的"金库楼"。
The Kui Tower

The four-storied brick tower, built in Ming Dynasty, is the highest building in the Residence. On the first floor there is a three meter well covered with a board. No strangers are admitted into the tower. This tower serves as a shelter to avoid unexpected incidents, but actually it is the treasury of the Residence.

照壁 相传为象麒麟但又不是麒麟，想象中的贪婪之兽，它拥有所有宝物，还想去吃太阳。此画在内宅门里墙上，为出内宅必走之路，用以告诫府人不要贪赃枉法。

Wall of Mirroring Tan

Tan, an imaginary beast which looks like a unicorn but not the same one. The beast is said to be so insatiable that it had all the treasures and even wanted to eat the sun. Hung on the wall of the Inner Residence, which is only path out the Inner Residence, the picture is used to warn people in the Confucius Residence of taking no bribes and bending no laws.

前上房 衍圣公接待至亲和近支族人、举行婚丧寿仪的地方。

The Front Main Room

The room is the place where Lord Yansheng met his close friends and his kinsfolk.

前上房内景
Inner View of Front Main Hall

前堂楼　　七间两层楼阁，清光绪十二年（公元 1886 年）重建，孔子 76 代孙"衍圣公"孔令贻及三位夫人陶氏、丰氏、王氏及两个女儿均住此楼。

The Tower of Front Hall

The seven-room, two-storied tower, renovated during the Qing Emperor Guangxu's reign, is the residence of Confucius's 76th descendants Lord Yiansheng and his three wives, Tao, Feng and Wang as well as their two daughters.

后堂楼院　　后堂楼院是孔德成的住宅。后堂楼为七间二层台楼，东西两侧各有五间二层配楼。

The Back Hall Tower

　　The seven-room, two-storied tower is the residence of Lord Kong Decheng. There are five subordinate towers flanking the eastern and western of the main tower.

王氏夫人室　孔子77代孙，"奉祀官"孔德成生母卧室。

Chamber of Lady Wang
　　Confucius's 77th grandson, Kong Decheng's mother's bedroom

孔德成婚房　现在仍保持着当年孔德成结婚时陈设布置。

Wedding Chamber of Kong Decheng and Sun Qifang
　　The chamber is still in the original layout of their wedding ceremony.

红萼轩　　任孔府西路。是当年衍圣公会客、读书和吟诗、习礼的地方，各种厅、堂、轩、房70余间，环境十分优雅别致。

Chamber for Red Calyx

It is found along the western path of the Residence. The western part is also the academy and is the place where Lord Yansheng met guests, studied, read poems and practiced rites. There are altogether 70 rooms, halls and chambers. It is a quiet and exquisite place. The Chamber of Red Calyx was the place where Lord Yan−Sheng practiced rites.

忠恕堂　孔府西路建筑，取《论语》"夫子之道，忠恕而已矣"语，是
衍圣公会集宾朋，燕居吟咏之处。

Hall of Fidelity and Generosity

　　Situated in the western part of the Residence and deriving it
name also from The Analects, the hall is the place where Lor
Yansheng held gatherings with his friends and recited poems.

红萼轩内景
Inner View of Chamber
for Red Calyx

西路北花厅
Courtyard of North Flowery Hall

后花园　在孔府的最后面，此园建于明代，园内有太湖石假山及各种奇花异草，特别是有一株五棵柏树环抱一棵槐树，十分奇特。

The Rear Garden

Situated in the innermost of the Residence and built in Ming Dynasty, the garden is very peculiar for the artificial rookeries, various exotic flowers and herb, and especially for the scholartree embraced by five cypresses.

五柏抱槐树 Hai Tree Embraced
By Five Cypresses

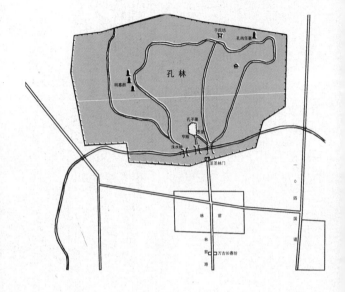

Map of Confucius Mausoleum

1. Everlasting Green Archway
2. Gate to the Saint
3. Second Gate to the Saint
4. Zhushui Bridge
5. Mausoleum of Confucius
6. The confucius Mausoleum
7. Mausoleums of Ming Dynasty
8. Mausoleum of Kong Shangren
9. Archway of lady Yu

孔　林

　　孔林位于曲阜城北，是孔子及其家族的专用墓地，也是目前世界上延时最久，面积最大的氏族墓地。孔林始于孔子死后第二年，随着孔子地位的日益提高，孔林的规模越来越大。自汉代以后，历代统治者对孔林重修、增修过13次，以至形成现在规模，总面积约2平方公里，周围林墙5.6公里，墙高3米多，厚1米。郭沫若曾说："这是一个很好的自然博物馆，也是孔氏家族的一部编年史"。孔林对于研究中国历代政治、经济、文化的发展以及丧葬风俗的演变也有着不可替代的作用。

The Confucius Mausoleum

　　Situated in the northwest of Qufu City, the Confucius Mausoleum, mausoleum for Confucius and his family, is the oldest and largest clan mausoleum in the world.It was first built in the year follwing Confucius's death and has been renovated later for many times since Han Dynasty with the increase of Confucius's social status. The Mausoleum covers a total area of about two square kilometers and was encircled by 5.6km long, 3 meter wide and 1 meter wide wall. Kuo Muoruo, a scholar in modern China, once said:"The Mausoleum is a perfect museum of nature, and also the annals of the Confucius." The mausoleum plays and implacable role in the research of the development of China's politics, economy and culture of the feudal society and the evolution of China's funeral practice.

万古长春坊 明万历二十二年（公元1594年）建。是曲阜现存最大的石坊。石坊两侧各有碑楼一座，记述大修孔林的情况。

The Everlasting Green Archway

　　It was built in the year 1594 and is the largest stone archway still in existence in Qufu. There are two arches on the two sides, recording the history of building the Mausoleum.

至圣林门 孔林大门，又称"大林门"，由大门和至圣林坊组成。大门建于元代，至圣林坊建于明代。

The Gate to the Saint

Also called the Great Mausoleum, the gate consists of the main gate and the archway. The main gate was built in Yuan Dynasty and the archway was built in Ming Dynasty.

二林门 建于元代,明、清时代重修。是一洞深邃城堡式拱门建筑,拱门上建有观楼。门洞上方篆书"至圣林"三字。

The Second Gate to the Mausoleum

Built in Yuan Dynasty and renovatde in Ming and Qing Dynasty, the gate is actually an archway of deep tunnel with a viewing stand on the top, in the middle of the archway there are three Chinese characters。"Zhi Sheng Lin" (To the Mausoleum).

洙水桥坊 洙水桥坊为洙水河而立，坊上"洙水桥"三字为明代严嵩所写。

The Archway of Zhushui Bridge

The Archway of Zhushui Bridge was built for the river, and the three Chinese characters "Zhu Shui Qiao"(The Bridge of ZhushuiRiver)were written by Yansong of Ming Dynasty.

孔子墓前墓道
The Path leeding to Confucius Tomb

香炉
The Incense Burner

子贡庐墓处 孔子墓西三间砖房为子贡庐墓处。孔子死后，众弟子守墓三年，独子贡守墓六年，实为尊师楷模。后人建房立石纪念。

Cottage of Mausoleum of Zigong

The cottage west of the mausoleum of Confucius is the mausoleum of Zigong, a disciple of Confucius , After the death of Confucius,his disciples guarded his mausoleum for three years, while Zigong guarded for six years,and set an example of respecting teachers. Later the cottage was built in memory of him.

孔子墓

孔子死后，弟子葬师时曾是"墓而不坟"，到秦汉时才将坟筑起。墓前一碑刻"大成至圣文宣王墓"，为明代正统八年（公元1443年）黄养正书。碑后还有一碑，刻"宣圣墓"三字，为蒙古乃马真后三年（公元1244年)立。

Mausoleum of Confucius

When Confucius died, his disciples buried him, but the Mausoleum was not built until the Qin and Han Dynasties. The inscriptions on the tombsdtone were written by Huang Yangzheng in 1448, and the inscriptions on the tablet be—hind was written by a Mongolian em—press in the year 1244.

楷 亭 传为孔子弟子子贡所植楷，后人立碑建亭以示纪念。
Jie Pavilion
It was said to be built by Zigong,a disciple of Confucius.

孔鲤墓　　孔子儿子墓，位于孔子墓东邻。
Mausoleum of KongLi

It is the mausoleum of Confucius's son and located to east the of the Mausoleum of Confucius.

孔伋墓　　孔子的孙子子思墓。子思，孟子的老师，曾作《中庸》，后被封为"述圣"墓前有石碑刻"三世祖墓"。
Mausolem of Kong Ji

It is the mausoleum of Confucius's grandson, Zisizi.Zisizi was the teacher of Menfucius and the author of The Doctrine of the Mean. On the tombstone there is inscriptions of "Mausoleum of three generations".

孔令贻墓 孔子76代孙"衍圣公墓"。
Mausoleum of Kong Lingyi

It is the mausoleum of the 76 generation of Confucius, Lord Yansheng.

孔尚任墓 清代著名剧作家、《桃花扇》作者孔尚任。
Mausoleum of Kong Shangren

It is the mausoleum of Kong Shangren, the famous dramatist of Fan of Peach Blossom.

于氏坊　为清朝皇帝乾隆之女立的纪念碑坊。
Archway of Lady Yu
　　It was built in memory of the daughter of Emperor of Qianlong of Qing Dynasty.

明墓群
Mausoleums of Ming Dynasty

汉画像石——围观捕鱼
The Fish man

汉画像石——扁鹊行医
Doctor Bian Que

夫子洞 　又称坤灵洞，相传为孔子出生处，位于尼山脚下，智源溪北岸石壁中。

Hole of Confucius

　　Also called Hole of Kunling and located at the foot of hill. The legend goes that it was the birth place of Confucius.

颜庙

祭祀颜子义颜无繇,为曲阜最早的宫殿式古建筑。

Temple of Yan Zi

Temple of Yan Zi,the eldest palacestyled building in Qufu,serves to offer a sacrifice to Yan Zi,or Yan Wuyiu,another name of his.

少昊陵　　位于曲阜城东 4 公里处。少昊相传为黄帝之子,宋时垒石为陵,有"中国金字塔"之称。

Emperor Shao Hao's Tomb

Four kilometers to the east of Qufu,The legond goes that Shao Hao was the son of Yellow Emperor and his mausoleum was built in Song Dynasty,which is also called "Pyramid of China".

寿丘 Shouqiu

万人愁碑
Wanrenchou Tablets

周公庙 位于曲阜城东北1里处，宋时在原太庙旧址立庙。明清多次维修，用于祭祀周公。孔子"入太庙，每事问"即指此处。
Temple of Lord Zhou

Temple of Lord Zhou,built on the original sitc of Ancient Temple in Song Dynasty and rebuilt many times during Ming and Qing dynasties,lies to the north east of Qufu and serves to offer a sacrifice to him.

洙泗书院　Zhusi Academy

洙泗书院本名讲堂，是孔子晚年的重要活动遗迹。孔子周游列国后，"自卫返鲁，于此删诗、序书、写礼乐、系周易"，边教学边整理古代典籍。

孟母林　Cenmetery of Mencius's　mother

石门山　　Shimen　Mountain

进曲阜坊　Gate Archway　to　Qufu

鹭鸶 （市鸟）
Heron （City Bird）

兰花 （市花）
Cymbidium (city flower)

九仙山　Jiuxian Mountain

论语碑苑
The Garden of
Confucius Analects

策　　划：丰　然　魏启新
主　　编：丰建伟　高玉忠
文　　字：陶　剑
摄　　影：陈　永
翻　　译：刘成干
美　　编：孔令军
印　　章：张继龙

孔子故乡全览　　孔孟故里丛书

出版发行：远方出版社
　　　　　（呼和浩特市新城区老缸房街18号）
经销：新华书店
印刷：山东省曲阜师范大学印刷厂
版次：2002年4月第1版
印次：2002年4月第1次印刷
开本：889×1194　1/48
印张：78　本册印张：2
字数：5000
印数：1—5000册
ISBN7-80595-537-9/I·231
价格：12.00元